P9-DBS-652

MACHINES ★ AT WORK

DUMP TRUCKS

BY CYNTHIA ROBERTS

THE CHILD'S WORLD® • MANKATO, MINNESOTA

The Child's World

Published in the United States of America by The Child's World®
1980 Lookout Drive • Mankato, MN 56003-1705
800-599-READ • www.childsworld.com

PHOTO CREDITS
© David M. Budd Photography: 4, 7, 8, 11, 12, 16, 19, 20
© iStockphoto.com/David Freund: cover, 2, 15
© iStockphoto.com/Tomasz Pietryszek: 3

ACKNOWLEDGMENTS
The Child's World®: Mary Berendes, Publishing Director;
Katherine Stevenson, Editor

The Design Lab: Kathleen Petelinsek, Design and Page Production

LIBRARY OF CONGRESS CATALOGING-IN-PUBLICATION DATA
Roberts, Cynthia, 1960–
  Dump trucks / by Cynthia Roberts.
    p. cm. — (Machines at work)
  Includes bibliographical references and index.
  ISBN 1-59296-830-9 (library bound : alk. paper)
  1. Dump trucks—Juvenile literature. I. Title. II. Series.
  TL230.15.R638 2006
  629.225—dc22   2006023289

9/08

e.l

 # Contents

This dump truck is leaving a building site. It is carrying dirt. ★

What are dump trucks?

Dump trucks are special kinds of **vehicles**. They carry loose things such as dirt, rocks, and sand. Then they tip them out. Most dump trucks are large. They can carry heavy loads.

How are dump trucks used?

Dump trucks are often used when people build things. Sometimes they carry **gravel** for building roads. Sometimes they bring dirt to fill in low places. Sometimes they carry away extra dirt or rocks.

Some dump trucks puff black smoke as they work. This one has a pipe on the side. You can see smoke coming out the top.

This driver runs the whole truck from the cab. He drives the truck from place to place. He works the dumper body, too.

What are the parts of a dump truck?

The front of the dump truck has a **cab**. The driver sits in the cab. The back of the truck has a dumper body. It holds the dirt or rocks.

How does a dump truck move?

A dump truck is a lot like other trucks. It has an **engine** that makes it move. The engine runs on **diesel fuel**. The engine makes power that turns the truck's wheels. The driver moves the truck from place to place.

Drivers must be careful! They must watch out for other machines.

A special machine is loading this dump truck. The machine scoops dirt and gravel into a bucket. It empties the bucket into the dumper body. ⭐

How do you load a dump truck?

A dump truck cannot load itself. Other machines fill the dumper body. They lift the dirt above the dumper body. Then they drop it in.

13

How does a dump truck dump?

Dump trucks unload themselves! Many of them work fairly simply. The worker uses the truck's **controls** to dump the load. A special part lifts the front of the dumper body. The dirt or rocks slide out the back.

14

★ This dump truck is dumping its load. The front of the dumper body lifts high. The load slides right out.

This big dump truck is carrying lots of dirt. How much do you think it weighs?

How much can a dump truck carry?

Dump trucks are made to carry big, heavy loads. The biggest can carry 20,000 pounds (9,072 kg). That is as much as 13 cows!

17

Are there different kinds of dump trucks?

There are many kinds of dump trucks. They come in different sizes and shapes. They have different kinds of dumper bodies. They have different ways of getting rid of their loads.

This truck's dumper body tips sideways. The load lands in a long pile.

 This dump truck is on its way to the next job.

Are dump trucks useful?

Dump trucks are very useful. They do lots of hard, dirty work. They are great for carrying rocks and other heavy loads. And they are very easy to unload. They are also fun to watch!

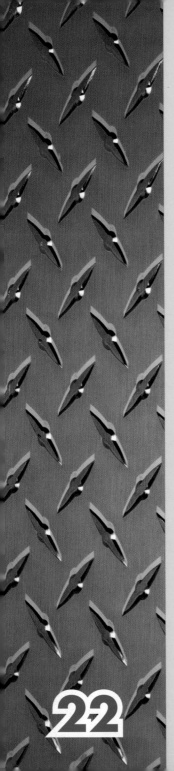

 # Glossary

cab (KAB) A machine's cab is the area where the driver sits.

controls (kun-TROHLZ) Controls are parts that people use to run a machine.

diesel fuel (DEE-sul fyool) Diesel fuel is a heavy oil that is burned to make power.

engine (EN-jun) An engine is a machine that makes something move.

gravel (GRA-vull) Gravel is loose, small stones.

vehicles (VEE-uh-kullz) Vehicles are things for carrying people or goods.

 # Books

Edwards, Julie Andrews, and Emma Walton Hamilton (illustrator). *Dumpy the Dump Truck.* New York: Hyperion Books, 2000.

Jango-Cohen, Judith. *Dump Trucks.* Minneapolis, MN: Lerner, 2003.

Mezzanotte, Jim. *Giant Dump Trucks.* Milwaukee, WI: Gareth Stevens, 2006.

Teitelbaum, Michael, and Uldis Klavins (illustrator). *If I Could Drive a Dump Truck!* New York: Scholastic, 2001.

Yardumian, Miryam, and Tibor Gergely (illustrator). *The Happy Man and His Dump Truck.* New York: Golden Books, 1978.

 # Web Sites

Visit our Web site for lots of links about dump trucks:
http://www.childsworld.com/links
Note to parents, teachers, and librarians: We routinely check our Web links to make sure they're safe, active sites—so encourage your readers to check them out!

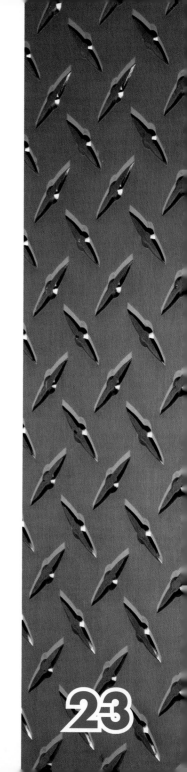

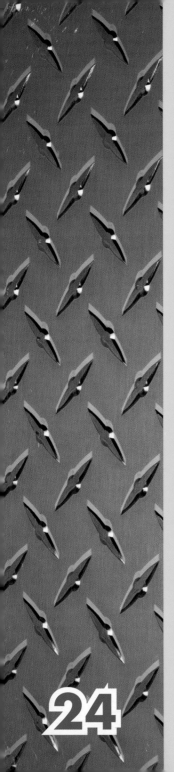

Index

About the Author

Even as a child, Cynthia Roberts knew she wanted to be a writer. She is always working to involve kids in reading and writing, and she loves spending time in the children's section of the library or bookstore. Cynthia enjoys gardening, traveling, and having fun with friends and family.